Passage Probabilities of Juvenile Chinook Salmon Through the Powerhouse and Regulating Outlet at Cougar Dam, Oregon, 2011

By John W. Beeman, Amy C. Hansen, Scott D. Evans, Philip V. Haner, Hal C. Hansel, and Collin D. Smith

Prepared in cooperation with the U.S. Army Corps of Engineers

Open-File Report 2012–1250

U.S. Department of the Interior
U.S. Geological Survey

U.S. Department of the Interior
KEN SALAZAR, Secretary

U.S. Geological Survey
Marcia K. McNutt, Director

U.S. Geological Survey, Reston, Virginia: 2012

For more information on the USGS—the Federal source for science about the Earth,
its natural and living resources, natural hazards, and the environment—visit
http://www.usgs.gov or call 1–888–ASK–USGS

For an overview of USGS information products, including maps, imagery, and publications,
visit *http://www.usgs.gov/pubprod*

To order this and other USGS information products, visit *http://store.usgs.gov*

Suggested citation:
Beeman, J.W., Hansen, A.C., Evans, S.E., Haner, P.V., Hansel, H.C., and Smith, C.D., 2012, Passage probabilities of
juvenile Chinook salmon through the powerhouse and regulating outlet at Cougar Dam, Oregon, 2011: U.S. Geological
Survey Open-File Report 2012-1250, 26 p.

Contents

Figures

Tables

Conversion Factors

Inch/Pound to SI

Multiply	By	To obtain
foot (ft)	0.3048	meter (m)
cubic foot (ft^3)	0.02832	cubic meter (m^3)
cubic foot per second (ft^3/s)	0.02832	cubic meter per second (m^3/s)

SI to Inch/Pound

Multiply	By	To obtain
millimeter (mm)	0.03937	inch (in.)
kilometer (km)	0.6214	mile (mi)
kilometer (km)	0.5400	mile, nautical (nmi)
liter (L)	0.2642	gallon (gal)
gram (g)	0.03527	ounce, avoirdupois (oz)

Temperature in degrees Celsius (°C) may be converted to degrees Fahrenheit (°F) as follows:
°F=(1.8×°C)+32

Vertical coordinate information is referenced to the National Geodetic Vertical Datum of 1929 (NGVD 29).

Horizontal coordinate information is referenced to the World Geodetic System of 1984 (WGS 84).

Passage Probabilities of Juvenile Chinook Salmon Through the Powerhouse and Regulating Outlet at Cougar Dam, Oregon, 2011

By John W. Beeman, Amy C. Braatz, Scott D. Evans, Philip V. Haner, Hal C. Hansel, and Collin D. Smith

Abstract

Cougar Dam near Springfield, Oregon, is one of several federally owned and operated flood-control projects within the Willamette Valley of western Oregon that were determined by the National Oceanic and Atmospheric Administration's National Marine Fisheries Service in 2008 to impact the long-term viability of several salmonid stocks. In response to this ruling, the U.S. Army Corps of Engineers is looking for means to reduce impacts to salmonids, including improving downstream passage of juvenile salmonids at Cougar Dam. This study of juvenile Chinook salmon (*Oncorhynchus tshawytscha*) passage at Cougar Dam was conducted to inform decisions about potential improvements for downstream fish passage. The primary objective of the study was to estimate route-specific passage probabilities of yearling Chinook salmon at Cougar Dam. The study was conducted using fish from a nearby hatchery surgically implanted with radio transmitters and passive integrated transponder (PIT) tags and released near the entrance of a temperature control tower through which all water going through the dam normally passes. Water passing through the temperature control tower may be routed through a penstock to a powerhouse with two Francis turbines, or to a spillway-like structure called the regulating outlet. Secondary objectives of the study were to estimate the probability that fish enter a bypass at a non-federal facility downstream, and to estimate dam-passage and in-river fish survival. Dam operating conditions during the study included an average forebay elevation of 1,580 feet (National Geodetic Vertical Datum of 1929) and an average of 48.2 percent of the total dam discharge of 1,106 cubic feet per second passing through a regulating outlet opening of 1.25 feet. Dam passage probability was greatest at night (0.8741 standard error [SE] 0.0265) and primarily through the regulating outlet (0.8896 SE 0.0617 day; 0.9417 SE 0.0175 night). The joint probability of entering the bypass at Leaburg Dam and being detected at the PIT system within the bypass was 0.0755 (SE 0.0363), but some fish were known to pass the PIT system undetected, indicating that the true probability of entering the bypass was underestimated. The estimated survival of fish passing through the temperature control tower, through the dam, and to a site at a bridge over the South Fork of the McKenzie River 3.9 kilometers downstream was 0.3680 (SE 0.1322) for fish passing through the powerhouse, and 0.4247 (SE 0.0440) for fish passing through the regulating outlet. The estimated in-river survival through the 37.3 kilometers from the bridge to a site at Leaburg Hatchery on the McKenzie River was 0.5857 (SE 0.2227) for fish that had passed through the powerhouse, and 0.4537 (SE 0.0551) for fish that had passed through the regulating outlet.

Introduction

The U.S. Army Corps of Engineers (USACE) operates the Willamette Project (Project) located in western Oregon, including Cougar Dam. The primary purpose of the Project is flood control, but it also is operated to provide hydroelectricity, irrigation water, navigation, instream flows for wildlife, and recreation. The Project includes 13 dams, about 68 km of revetments, and several fish hatcheries. Cougar Dam, and several other dams, are located on tributaries of the Willamette River. A recent Biological Opinion determined that the Project jeopardizes the sustainability of anadromous fish stocks in the Willamette River Basin (National Oceanic and Atmospheric Administration, 2008).

Cougar Dam is a 158-m-tall rock-fill dam on the South Fork of the McKenzie River, located about 63 km east of Springfield, Oregon. The dam, completed in 1964, is owned and operated by the USACE. It has a hydraulic capacity of 1,050 ft³/s and two Francis turbine units capable of generating a total of 25 megawatts. The dam also has a spillway with Tainter gates, and a temperature control tower installed in 2005 that passes water to a flow-regulating outlet (RO) and to a powerhouse penstock. The reservoir primarily is used for flood control, and as such, the forebay elevation is maintained at high elevations during summer months and low elevations during winter months. Maximum conservation pool elevation of 1,690 ft National Geodetic Vertical Datum of 1929 (NGVD29) typically is reached in May, and a minimum flood-control pool elevation of 1,532 ft NGVD29 is usually reached in December. A temperature control tower allows the use of water from various depths in the forebay to provide water temperatures suitable for salmon in areas downstream of the dam. During normal conditions, all water passing through the dam enters the temperature control tower and passes to the tailrace either through the RO intake at elevation 1,478 ft NGVD29, or through the powerhouse penstock intake at elevation 1,420 ft NGVD29 (fig. 1). A newly constructed fish ladder and trapping facility are used to collect adult salmon in the tailrace for transportation upstream, and provide a means of upstream passage for adult salmon. There is currently no passage route designed for downstream passage of juvenile salmon.

The 2008 Willamette Biological Opinion requires improvements to operations and structures to reduce impacts on Upper Willamette River (UWR) Chinook salmon (*Oncorhynchus tshawytscha*) and UWR steelhead (*O. mykiss*; National Oceanic and Atmospheric Administration, 2008). Among these improvements is a requirement to provide safe downstream passage for juvenile salmonids, a goal that may be achieved through operational or structural alternatives. Information about the probabilities of fish passage and survival through the RO and penstock routes can be used to inform decisions about downstream passage alternatives.

Few studies of the passage and survival of fish traveling through the temperature control tower had been conducted at Cougar Dam at the time of this report. Normandeau and Associates, Inc., used fish tagged with a Hi-Z Turb-N-tag (balloon tag) and a radio tag to estimate the direct survival of yearling Chinook salmon of hatchery origin during several dam operating conditions (Monzyk and others, 2011a). They found lower survival of fish passing through the powerhouse compared to those passing through the RO. Their preliminary estimates of survival 48-h post-passage ranged from 36.4 to 42.4 percent for fish passing through the powerhouse, and 84.6 to 88.3 percent for fish passing through the RO, depending on the operating conditions. They also noted that the results may have been compromised by premature inflation of the tag balloons due to the long passage times at this dam compared to most others (4–6 min versus less than 2 min). Duncan (2011) passed sensor packages through the two routes and found more severe conditions within the powerhouse route than in the RO route, corroborating the results described in Monzyk and others (2011a). Monzyk and others (2011b) used fish implanted with half-duplex passive integrated transponder (PIT) tags to estimate the passage percentages of yearling Chinook salmon of hatchery origin through the powerhouse and RO routes during two dam operating conditions. They estimated that 51 percent of the fish passed through the RO when the dam discharge was 530 ft³/s through the RO and 1,060 ft³/s through the powerhouse, and that 64.3 percent passed through the RO when dam discharge was 2,700 ft³/s through the RO and 1,080 ft³/s through the powerhouse. They noted several potential biases in their study, including high variation in the detection probabilities of live and dead fish, reliance on survival results from the studies of balloon-tagged fish to determine the proportion of live and dead fish for adjusting detection probabilities, and low overall detection probabilities.

The study described in this report was designed to estimate several passage, survival, and detection probabilities of juvenile Chinook salmon passing through the dam. The primary objective was to estimate the route-specific passage proportions at the penstock and RO routes during an operation of nearly equal discharge through each route. As originally designed, the secondary objective of the study was to estimate the detection probability of the PIT detection system at Leaburg Dam on the McKenzie River 47 river kilometers (rkm) downstream of Cougar Dam. As a tertiary objective, the study design was altered slightly based on comments received during peer review of the proposal to also enable estimates of fish survival.

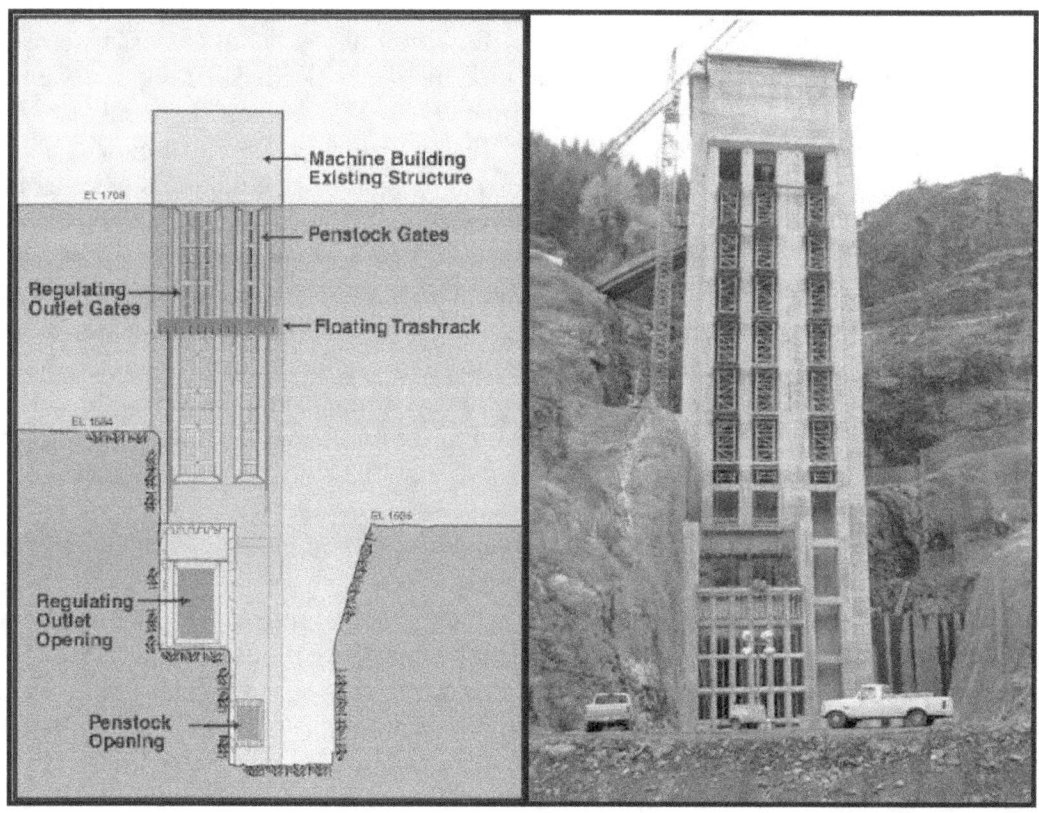

Figure 1. Schematic and photograph of the temperature control tower in the forebay of Cougar Dam, Oregon. Schematic and photograph are from the U.S. Army Corps of Engineers.

Methods

Fish Capture, Handling, Tagging, and Release

The data described in this report were collected from yearling juvenile Chinook salmon carrying radio transmitters (hereafter referred to as tags) and PIT tags. The tagged fish were of hatchery origin and were from the McKenzie River Hatchery in Leaburg, Oregon.

Approximately 1,000 hatchery fish were sorted by size at McKenzie River Hatchery and placed into an indoor tank in August 2011 to meet a minimum fork-length requirement of 95 mm for both this study and a concurrent study of fish movements in the reservoir based on acoustic telemetry techniques. The tank was supplied with flowing river water. On each of four dates in November 2011, fish were netted from the raceway, placed into a 264 L transport tank, and taken to the tagging site at the Cougar Dam adult fish facility where they were held between 20.3 and 26.1 h prior to tagging. The recommendations from the Surgical Protocol Steering Committee (2011) were followed in all aspects of the fish holding, tagging, and releasing procedures. There was one surgeon.

Tag implantation and fish recovery were completed at the Cougar Dam adult fish facility. Fish were considered suitable for tagging if they were free of major injuries, had no external signs of gas bubble trauma or fungus, and were less than or equal to 20 percent descaled. To implant the tag, fish were anesthetized using buffered tricane methanesulfonate (MS-222, Argent Chemical Laboratories, Redmond, Washington) at a concentration of 80 mg/L. Fish weight and length were measured immediately prior to surgery. All weighing, measuring, and containment equipment were treated with a 0.25 ml/L concentration of Stress Coat (Aquarium Pharmaceuticals, Inc., Chalfont, Pennsylvania) to reduce handling-related stress to the fish via electrolyte loss. Fish were placed in a 19 L perforated recovery bucket filled with 7 L of river water immediately after surgery. Dissolved oxygen levels were maintained between 80 and 100 percent of saturation during recovery. Each recovery bucket held up to three fish. Fish were watched periodically during the first 10 mins after surgery to ensure they recovered from anesthesia. Recovery buckets were then fitted with lids and placed in a raceway provided with flowing river water, where fish were held for 24.0–27.2 h prior to release. The recovery buckets were floated in the raceway using rubber inner tubes fastened around the top to allow fish access to air in order to adjust their buoyancy.

Tagged fish were released daily near 1:00 PM and 6:00 PM on November 8-11, 2011at the upstream face of the middle temperature control tower trash rack. To prepare for fish releases, the recovery buckets were removed from the raceway, inspected for mortalities and functioning radio tags, and transferred into an insulated 1,556 L plastic tank. Two tanks were mounted on a flatbed trailer with lids to limit the amount of water spilling out during transport. River water was placed into each tank and the fish and recovery buckets were added and driven to the boat ramp at the earthen dam. Recovery buckets were then transferred onto a boat and taken to a floating platform at the southeastern corner of the temperature control tower. Water-quality measurements were recorded to ensure the water temperature difference between the recovery bucket and the reservoir was not greater than 2 C, which would require tempering per the Surgical Protocols Steering Committee (2011). Fish were released by gently pouring the recovery-bucket contents into a conical-bottom tank provided with flowing reservoir water connected to 10 m of a 5.1-cm-diameter polyvinyl chloride pipe that terminated about 1 m deep in front of the middle trash rack (fig. 2).

Radio Tags

The radio tags used in this study had dimensions in mm of 10 long × 5 wide × 3 deep; mass (g) = 0.31 in air, and they had a 16-cm trailing antenna (Lotek Wireless model NTQ-2, Newmarket, Ontario, Canada). Typical tag life, as stated by the manufacturer, was expected to be between 13.6 and 16.0 days given the transmission intervals of the tags, which were 1.7, 1.8, 1.9, and 2.0 s. Several transmission intervals were used to increase the probability of detection if many tags were in the same detection field together. The tags were nearly equally divided among operating frequencies of 166.300, 166.340, 166.360, and 166.380 MHz and emitted pulse-coded transmissions. A 23 mm long full-duplex PIT-tag weighing 0.10 g was placed inside the body cavity along with the radio tag.

Figure 2. Photographs of fish release system used to deliver fish in front of the trash rack, Cougar Reservoir, Oregon, 2011. Photographs taken by Matthew Sholtis of the U.S. Geological Survey, 2011.

Radio-Telemetry Detection Systems

Radio-telemetry receiving systems were installed at the temperature control tower, in the dam tailraces, and at several sites downstream (figs. 3 and 4). Stripped coaxial cable antennas (Beeman and others, 2004) were hung underwater approximately 3-m-deep inside the temperature control tower to enable estimation of the time fish entered and exited the temperature control tower. Detection systems in the powerhouse and RO tailraces were 'double array' systems providing two independent detection systems from which to estimate detection probabilities at each passage route. Each array consisted of three 3-element Yagi antennas providing a single combined input into two SRX-400 or SRX-600 receivers (Lotek Wireless) and one Orion receiver (Sigma8, Newmarket, Ontario, Canada). The SRX receivers are of the narrow-band type and sequentially scanned each of the four tag frequencies for 2.5 s. The Orion receiver is a wide-band type and scanned the four frequencies nearly simultaneously. Radio-telemetry detection systems downstream of the dam tailraces each consisted of one narrow-band receiver with an input from two Yagi antennas. They were installed at the South Fork McKenzie River Bridge crossing Aufderheide Road, Leaburg Hatchery, and McKenzie River Hatchery. These sites were 93.2, 55.9, and 52.7 km from the mouth of the Willamette River and were 3.9, 41.2, and 44.6 km downstream of Cougar Dam. The radio signals traveling from the Yagi antennas to the receivers were amplified near the antennas and attenuated near the receivers to minimize transmission losses. Data from the receivers were downloaded on a frequency commensurate with the amount of data they were recording (usually daily).

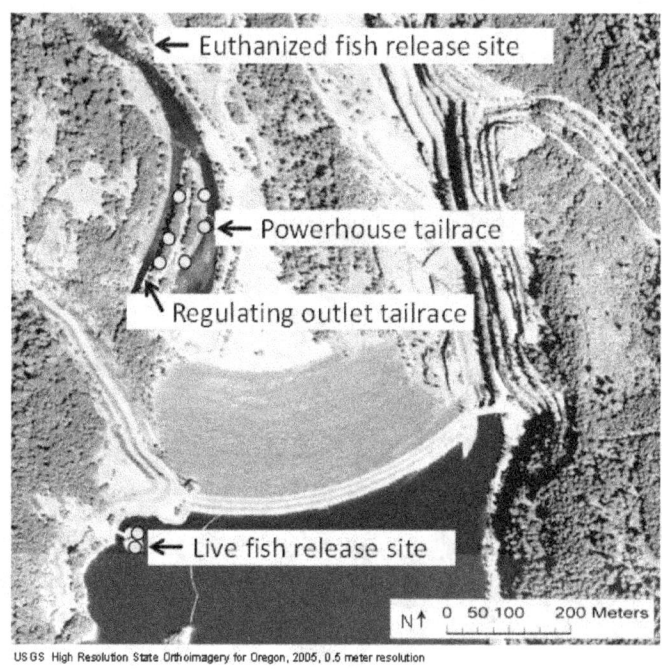

Figure 3. Locations of radio-telemetry antennas (yellow circles) deployed at the temperature control tower at Cougar Dam and in the regulating outlet tailrace and powerhouse tailrace.

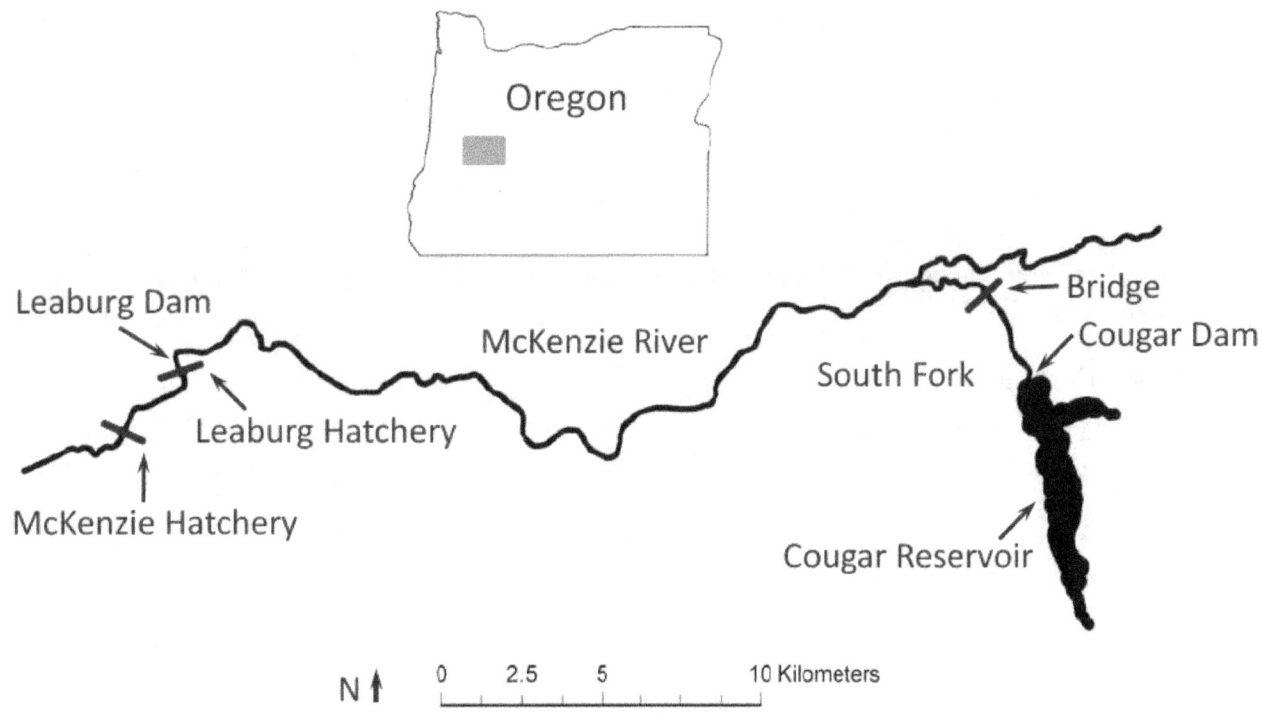

Figure 4. Schematic of radio-telemetry antenna locations (short lines) deployed on the South Fork McKenzie River and the main stem McKenzie River.

PIT-Tag Detection System at Leaburg Dam

The full-duplex PIT-detection system in the screened smolt-bypass channel at Leaburg Dam is on the western side of the McKenzie River slightly downstream of Leaburg Dam and consists of three coils. The site is owned and operated by the Eugene Water and Electric Board. Further information about the detection system is available at http://www.ptagis.org/ under the site code LEA.

Data Management and Analysis

Removing False-Positive Records

Records from the radio-telemetry receivers suspected of being false-positive detections were removed prior to analysis. False-positive detections are those that indicate presence of a tag when it is not present; they are possible in all telemetry systems. False-positive detections occur when telemetry receivers decode a transmission that matches a valid tag. Common causes of false-positive detections are overlapping transmissions of multiple tags at one time creating a pattern of another tag that is not present, and ambient noise doing the same, with or without the presence of telemetry tags. Several commonly used steps were implemented to reduce the probability of false-positive detections in the data (Skalski and others, 2002; Beeman and Perry, 2012). First, only records from tags released as part of this study occurring after their time of release were retained. After that step, the criteria were dependent on the type of telemetry receiver and its location. Records from wide-band receivers in the dam tailraces were retained if they had a received signal strength (as recorded by the receiver) of -105 decibels relative to an isotropic radiator (dBi) and there were at least three consecutive detections consistent with the tag repetition rate. Data from narrow-band receivers in the temperature control tower and dam tailraces were retained if they had a minimum received power of at least 50 (on a unitless receiver-measured scale of about 15–250) and were within 1 min of another record at the same site. Data from narrow-band receivers at sites downstream of the dam tailraces were treated similarly, but required a minimum receiver power of 30, because they were in areas with less ambient radio noise than the dam tailraces. Lastly, records were only retained if they were consistent with a geographical movement in a downstream direction among sites. The series of steps are similar to those of "Method B" described by Beeman and Perry (2012).

Assigning Passage Route

The route of passage was assigned based on the location and time of the first detection of fish at the radio-telemetry arrays in the powerhouse tailrace or RO tailrace. Fish that were not detected by radio-telemetry arrays in the tailraces but were captured in rotary screw traps in the tailraces were not assigned a passage route based on the trap location, because some study fish moved between tailraces prior to traveling downstream, which indicated that capture in a trap was not an absolute measure of their route of passage.

Estimating Travel Times

The time elapsed between and among detection sites was described using Kaplan-Meier survivorship functions (Hosmer and Lemeshow, 1999). The travel time between any two detection sites was estimated as the time from the last detection at the upstream site to the first detection at the downstream site. The survivorship function of a variable T is defined as

$$S(t) = \Pr\{T > t\}, \tag{1}$$

where T is a random variable with a probability distribution, denoting an event time for an individual. If the event of interest is passing a particular site, the survivorship function gives the probability of not passing the site after time t. As such, the median time occurs when the survivorship function equals 0.5. In the absence of censoring, the survivorship function represents the proportion of the population that has not experienced an event (for example, passing a site). Examining the survivorship function can be useful to describe the timing of events as well as the proportion of the population still at risk of the event at different points in time. Incomplete detection histories were right censored at the last time of detection at the nearest upstream site (Hosmer and Lemeshow, 1999).

Estimating Passage, Detection, and Survival Probabilities

Cormack-Jolly-Seber (CJS) mark-recapture methods were used to estimate passage, detection, and survival probabilities (Cormack, 1964; Jolly, 1965; Seber, 1965). Detection of a tagged animal is the product of the probability of presence and the probability of detection, so these parameters must be separately estimated. A modification of the Route-Specific Survival Model (RSSM) of Skalski and others (2002) was used to estimate passage, detection, and survival parameters of interest. The mathematical model was modified to reflect a single-release design rather than a paired-release design, because we did not release live tagged fish downstream of the dam. Parameters of interest and profile-likelihood confidence intervals were estimated using maximum-likelihood techniques with the User-Specified Estimation Routine software (version 4.7.0, Fletch Quasi-Newton optimizer; Lady and Skalski, 2009).

8

The single-release design was used to estimate survival of fish through the various study reaches and through the entire study area. The term "single-release" refers to the use of one or more releases of fish made at a single location. The minimum requirements for this design are (1) tagged fish are uniquely identifiable, (2) at least two detection sites exist downstream of the release location, (3) all or some of the marked fish recaptured at each detection location are re-released, and (4) the identities of the marked fish recaptured at each location are recorded. There are two primary potential biases associated with this design. The first is that the expression of mortality due to tagging or handling cannot be separated from other sources of mortality. These may be separated using other designs, including the paired-release design of Burnham and others (1987). The second is that the live/dead status of tagged fish must be correctly assigned. Bias can arise if fish-passage times through the study area exceed tag life, or if dead fish with live tags are detected. These possibilities may be evaluated by conducting tag-life experiments using a subset of the tags and comparing those distributions to fish travel-time distributions, and by releasing euthanized fish with live tags near the tailrace of the dam. Inasmuch as estimating survival was not the primary objective of this study, we used the manufacturer's advertised tag life as the expected life of the tags in this study rather than conducting a tag-life study. We did release euthanized tagged fish slightly downstream of the convergence of the powerhouse and regulating outlet tailraces by gently tossing them from the riverbank into the middle of the river. These fish were euthanized by an overdose in MS-222, severing gill arches, and pithing as described in Beeman and others (2010).

The survival estimated in this and other studies in which the fate of animals is not directly observed is termed "apparent survival." Apparent survival is the probability that an animal remains available for recapture, or more specifically "detection," in the context of this study. In this study, it is the joint probability that the animal is alive and migrates through the study area. As such, fish that leave the study area undetected and do not return, or stop migrating downstream, are counted as mortalities. Fish remaining within the study area after their tags cease operating also are counted as mortalities.

Summarized detection histories make up the basic input for the mark-recapture model and are used in the estimation procedure. In general, the passage, detection, and survival probabilities are derived by estimating the probability of each possible detection from the observed frequencies of each detection history, and using maximum-likelihood methods to find parameter estimates of survival, passage, and detection probabilities that are most likely to occur, given the observed data. The RSSM uses a primary likelihood to estimate survival and passage probabilities, and auxiliary likelihoods to estimate independent route-specific detection probabilities. The auxiliary likelihoods are based on detections at a primary and secondary detection array in each tailrace, commonly referred to as a 'double array'. In the detection history, the data from these arrays are located in columns 2 and 3 of table 1. The detection probabilities at sites downstream of the dam tailraces were assumed to be equal for fish passing the dam during day and night periods, and for fish passing through the RO and powerhouse routes.

Passage and survival probabilities were estimated with one mathematical model, and the joint probability of entering and being detected at the PIT-tag detection system in the Leaburg Dam bypass was estimated with another. Separate models were used because fish passing Leaburg Dam could be detected within the bypass but the study design did not enable detection of fish passing Leaburg Dam at the spillway. Using a separate model to estimate the passage and survival probabilities—which was the primary objective of the study—avoided the confounding of parameters and additional assumptions required if survival between the Leaburg Dam bypass and the radio-telemetry detection site at Leaburg Hatchery were estimated with a single model. Schematics of the two models are in appendixes A and B.

Table 1. Descriptions of columns in the detection histories of radio and PIT-tagged yearling Chinook salmon released during this study.

[Columns 2 and 3 of the detection histories represent detection sites in the regulating outlet (RO) or powerhouse (PH) tailraces. Column 5 was used for estimation of the joint probability of entering the Leaburg Dam diversion bypass and being detected by the PIT detection system there, but was omitted for estimation of passage and survival probabilities]

Column	Definition	Possible values
1	Release of live fish with functioning tag	1
2	Primary tailrace radio-telemetry array	RO, PH, UN (undetected)
3	Secondary tailrace radio-telemetry array	RO, PH, UN (undetected)
4	Radio-telemetry array at South Fork McKenzie River bridge	1 (detected), 0 (undetected)
5	PIT detector at Leaburg Dam diversion	1 (detected), 0 (undetected)
6	Radio-telemetry array near Leaburg Fish Hatchery	1 (detected), 0 (undetected)
7	Radio-telemetry array near McKenzie River Fish Hatchery or PIT detection systems downstream	1 (detected), 0 (undetected)

Initial model outputs indicated that more fish were detected at downstream detection arrays than would be expected given the route-specific detection probabilities estimated from the double arrays in each tailrace route. There were 30 tagged fish that were known to have passed the dam tailraces without being detected there (N=27 for the analysis of dam passage and survival probabilities, in which fish detected in the Leaburg PIT system were omitted). This indicated there was potentially a zone, or multiple zones, in one or both tailraces with poor coverage by the telemetry arrays, or that there was a high incidence of collisions among tag signals preventing them from being detected. The broad coverage by the telemetry arrays was similar in each tailrace and was not suspected as a factor. We therefore modified the RSSM model to estimate the route-specific detection probability of the RO tailrace arrays using the CJS method based on detections downstream rather than the double array. The telemetry receivers collected much more data from the RO tailrace than the powerhouse tailrace and filled some receiver memories on several occasions, suggesting many more fish passed the RO route than the powerhouse route, which is consistent with a higher probability of collisions among tags in the RO tailrace.

Results

Fish Capture, Handling, Tagging, and Release

A total of 295 hatchery fish were tagged and released from November 8 to 11, 2011. The average fork length was 132.4 mm (range 102.0–166.0 mm), and the average weight was 26.1 g (range 12.1–52.6 g; tables 2 and 3). The tag-weight to body-weight ratio based on the 0.41 g weight of the radio tag plus the PIT tag ranged from 0.78 to 3.39 percent with an average of 1.57 percent. There were no mortalities in the pre-tag or post-tag holding periods.

Several fish were omitted prior to analysis. These included four with radio tags not heard during release or thereafter, four that were collected in screw traps in the tailrace but not at radio-telemetry sites nearby, and three that were detected passing the dam after the study treatment operation had ended. In addition, radio-telemetry detections after collection in a rotary screw trap or PIT detection were omitted from analyses of travel time and survival, because they experienced events unlike those of the other fish. The analyses were therefore based on a total of 261 live fish released, and 23 euthanized fish released.

Table 2. Summary statistics of fork length (mm) and weight (g) of radio- and PIT-tagged yearling Chinook salmon at Cougar Reservoir, Oregon, 2011.

[SD is standard deviation]

Release date and time	Fork length				Weight		
	N	Mean	SD	Range	Mean	SD	Range
Nov. 08 2011 13:40:00	35	131.7	15.74	102–166	25.9	9.2	12.9–52.6
Nov. 08 2011 18:43:00	34	129.4	15.18	110–158	24.5	8.7	14.6–42.9
Nov. 09 2011 13:15:00	34	130.1	16.88	110–166	24.9	9.7	14.1–52.2
Nov. 09 2011 18:21:00	35	132.1	16.50	107–160	26.0	9.2	13.7–43.3
Nov. 10 2011 12:55:00	34	136.6	17.60	102–158	28.7	9.5	12.4–41.8
Nov. 10 2011 18:11:00	33	134.5	14.73	113–164	27.0	8.0	16.2–46.4
Nov. 11 2011 12:13:00	34	129.2	14.39	107–159	24.0	7.6	13.7–40.7
Nov. 11 2011 18:16:00	32	136.1	13.43	111–158	28.0	7.7	13.7–44.2

Table 3. Summary statistics of fork length (mm) and weight (g) of euthanized radio- and PIT-tagged yearling Chinook salmon released at the Cougar Dam tailrace, Oregon, 2011.

[SD is standard deviation]

Release date and time	Fork length				Weight		
	N	Mean	SD	Range	Mean	SD	Range
Nov. 08 2011 12:33:00	6	128.8	15.61	102–144	23.6	6.7	12.1–29.5
Nov. 09 2011 17:45:00	6	132.0	14.78	115–149	25.1	7.0	16.7–33.5
Nov. 10 2011 12:25:00	6	132.8	16.90	112–157	26.7	10.4	15.7–43.5
Nov. 11 2011 19:07:00	6	135.5	13.52	119–156	27.0	7.2	18.5–39.4

Environmental Conditions and Dam Operations

Cougar Dam operations were consistent during the passage times of radio-tagged juvenile Chinook salmon. From November 8 through 17, the mean daily discharge through the powerhouse was 0.57 thousand ft^3/s (range 0.56–0.59 thousand ft^3/s), and the mean daily discharge through the RO was 0.53 thousand ft^3/s (range 0.52–0.53 thousand ft^3/s; fig. 5). The RO gate opening was 1.25 ft. Mean daily forebay elevation and head over the weir gates declined during the 10-day evaluation period (forebay elevation mean 1,579.78 ft NGVD29, range 1,571.78–1,587.61 ft NGVD29; head mean 17.59 ft, range 10.19–26.02 ft). Daily mean temperature for the top 13–18 ft of water measured at the temperature control tower averaged 7.23°C (range 6.53–8.42°C).

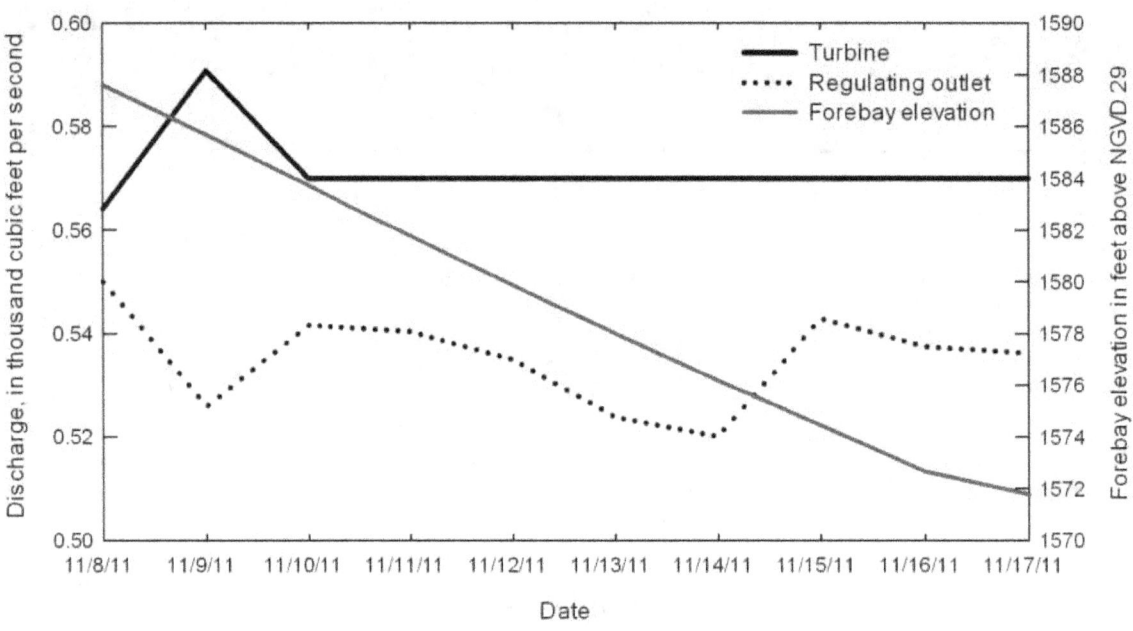

Figure 5. Daily average discharge through the powerhouse and regulating outlet (left vertical axis) and forebay elevation (right vertical axis) at Cougar Dam during passage of radio-tagged yearling Chinook salmon at Cougar Dam, Oregon, 2011.

Timing of Dam Passage

Most fish passed through the temperature-control tower during the night. This pattern was similar for fish released during the day (light bars on fig. 6) and those released at night (dark bars on fig. 6). Nearly equal numbers of fish passing the dam were released during the light (47.1 percent, $N=80$) and dark periods (52.9 percent, $N=90$). Overall, 13.5 percent ($N=23$) of fish passed during the light, and 86.5 percent ($N=147$) passed during the dark. Most fish (54.1 percent ; $N=92$) passed during the dusk crepuscular period between 5:00 p.m. and 7:00 p.m. (fig. 6) and 78.8 percent ($N=34$) passed between midnight and 5:00 a.m.

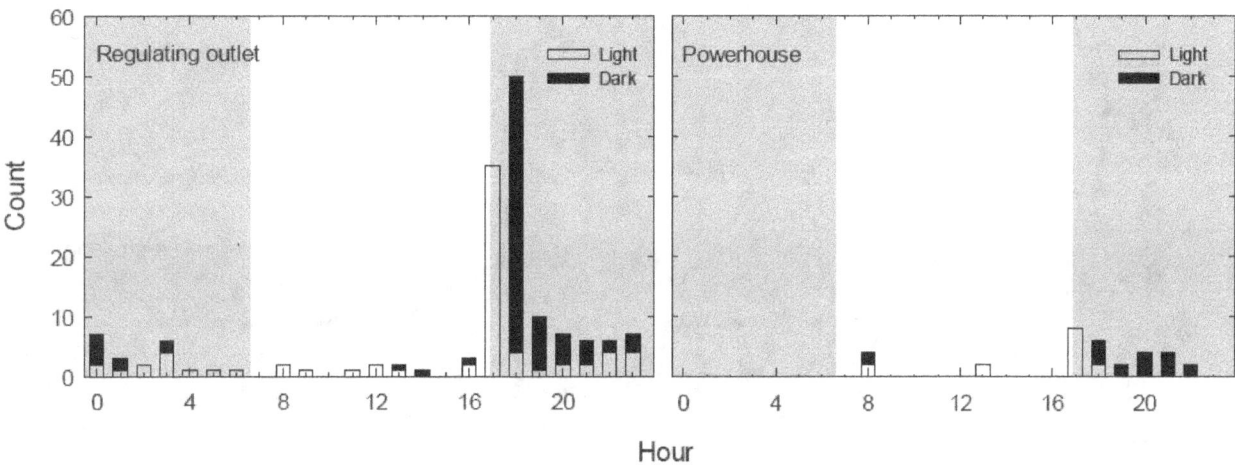

Figure 6. Hour of known passage of radio-tagged yearling Chinook salmon (*N*=170) at Cougar Dam, Oregon, 2011. Bar shading indicates diel period at release. Background shading indicates diel period of dam passage as indicated by the first detection in the tailrace (shading represents 5:17 p.m. to 6:30 a.m.).

Travel Times

Travel times of fish passing through the RO and those passing through the powerhouse generally were similar, but few fish passed through the powerhouse (fig. 7). The median time from release to last detection in the tower was 3.71 h (*N* =160, range 0.01–262.07 h). Some fish entered the tower after release and then returned to the forebay prior to passage. The median times from last detection in the tower to the first detection in the tailrace were 0.20 h for fish detected passing through the RO (*N* =101, range 0.04–188.78 h), and 0.33 h for fish that passed through the powerhouse (*N* =11, range 0.00–53.09 h). From the tailrace to the South Fork McKenzie River Bridge, travel times were longer for fish that passed through the RO than fish that passed through the powerhouse, though there were few fish passing the powerhouse for comparison. Median travel times from the RO to the bridge site were 4.53 h (*N*=60, range 3.11–56.30 h), while powerhouse to the bridge was 1.46 h (*N*=6, range 0.60–2.88 h). Few fish were detected passing the last two sites, so we combined the two passage routes for travel time summaries to those sites. The median travel time over the 37.3 km from the South Fork McKenzie River bridge to Leaburg Hatchery was 29.00 h (*N*=32, range 7.96–248.67 h). The median travel time over the 3.9 km from Leaburg Hatchery to McKenzie River Hatchery was 1.18 h (*N*=33, range 0.57–23.02 h). The median travel time over the 41.2 km from release to the McKenzie River Hatchery was 51.02 h (*N*=38, range 16.14–257.53 h). Three fish were detected at PIT detection sites well after the battery in the radio tag was expected to have expired (see next section). Eight fish were detected at the PIT detection system within the Leaburg Canal bypass, and another 10 were captured in the screw trap within the bypass. Two fish were also detected at the PIT detection system in the Walterville Canal bypass.

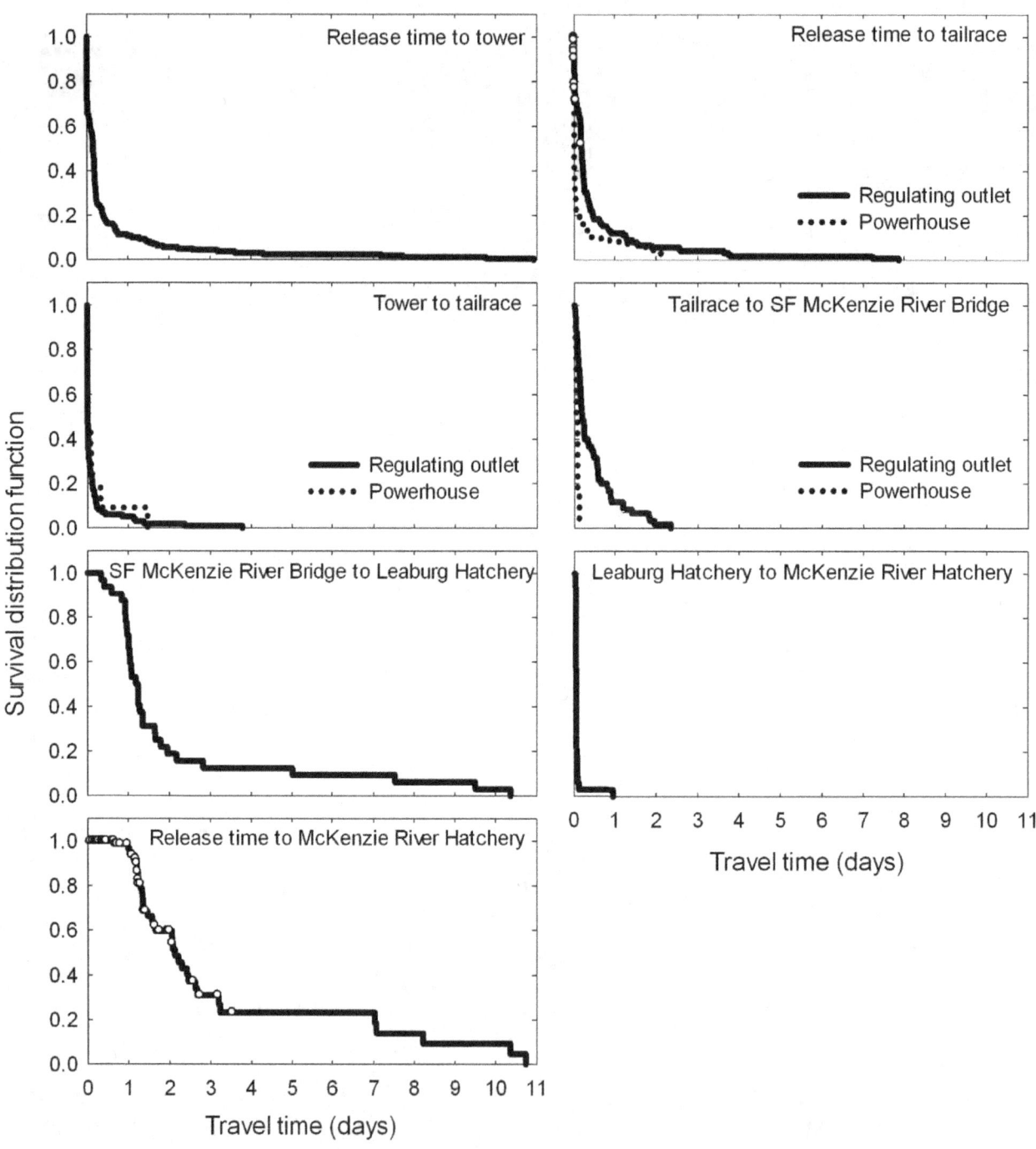

Figure 7. Travel times of radio-tagged yearling Chinook salmon released at Cougar Dam, Oregon, November 2011. Black solid lines represent fish that passed through the regulating outlet, and dotted lines represent fish that passed through the powerhouse. Circles represent censored observations.

Estimates of Passage, Detection, and Survival Probabilities

The estimates of passage and survival probabilities were based on detection histories of 261 live, tagged fish released minus the 18 fish that were detected within the diversion bypass at Leaburg Dam. Fish passing through the bypass at Leaburg Dam were omitted because they were exposed to a different environment than the fish passing Leaburg Dam without entering the diversion, and may have had a different survival after passage than fish that did not enter the bypass. The most common detection histories were of fish undetected downstream after release ($N = 60$), fish detected passing the RO at night and never detected again ($N = 76$), and fish detected passing the RO at night and detected downstream ($N = 49$; appendix C). The $N = 60$ tagged fish undetected downstream after release were assumed to have passed the dam, because they were no longer detected within the tower and were not subsequently detected in the forebay near the tower; many of these fish were detected within the temperature control tower after release. The estimated probability of study fish passage at the dam was 0.9142 (SE 0.0519). The mean size of fish passing through the RO was 132.9 mm fork length (range 102–164 mm) and 26.35 g weight (range 12.9–46.4 g). The mean size of fish passing through the powerhouse was 128.2 mm length (range 102–155 mm) and 24.08 g weight (range 12.4–44.2 g).

No euthanized tagged fish were detected downstream of the dam tailrace, but there was evidence of live fish passing detection sites with dead radio tags. The lack of detections of euthanized tagged fish suggests there were no false-positive detections due to dead fish with live tags. False-positive detections result in survival estimates that are biased upward, but this was not supported by the data. There were three tagged fish that were detected at PIT detection sites after their radio tags were expected to have died (expected tag life was 13.6–16.0 days, depending on the tag repetition rate), indicating the presence of false negatives in the data. One of these fish was detected in the Leaburg Dam bypass on December 5, 2011, at 01:40:56 (the first of three detections), another was detected at Willamette Falls Dam on December 17, 2011, at 10:52:38, and the last was detected at the Leaburg Dam bypass on January 24, 2012, at 22:47:29 (based on data in the http://www.ptagis.org database as of October 16, 2012). The first of these fish was last detected via radio-telemetry at the RO tailrace, and the other two were last detected at the McKenzie River Bridge. False negative detections result in survival estimates that are biased low. We did not estimate the extent of the bias due to the small number of fish in this category and the unknown detection probabilities of the PIT sites.

Route-Specific Passage Probabilities

Dam passage was primarily through the RO and primarily at night. Passage probabilities through the RO were 0.8896 (SE 0.0617) during the day and 0.9417 (SE 0.0175) during the night (table 4). The estimated overall passage probability at night when data from both routes was pooled was 0.8741 (SE 0.0265). The overall RO passage probability when data from day and night are pooled is 0.9352 (SE 0.1722), meaning that about 94 percent of the tagged fish passed through the RO and the remainder (about 6 percent) passed through the powerhouse.

Passage and Detection Probability at the Leaburg PIT Detector

The estimate of the passage and detection probability at the Leaburg PIT detector was 0.0755 (SE 0.0363). It represents the joint probability that the study fish in the McKenzie River passed through the diversion bypass and were detected at the PIT tag detector system. We did not separately estimate the detection probability of the PIT tag detector system once fish were in the diversion. There were another 10 fish from this study that were sampled in the screw trap within the diversion that were not detected at the PIT detector, which is upstream of the trap. This provides evidence that the detection probability of the PIT detector was no greater than 0.44 (8÷18) during the period of this study. The detection history table used for this analysis is in appendix D.

Route-Specific Survival

Route-specific survival was similar for fish passing through the RO and powerhouse. The estimate of survival from entry into the temperature control tower to the South Fork McKenzie River bridge 3.9 km downstream of the dam was 0.4247 (SE 0.0440) for fish passing through the RO and 0.3680 (SE 0.1322) for fish passing through the powerhouse. The standard error of the powerhouse estimate is large relative to the RO estimate due to the small number of fish passing through the powerhouse (11 tagged fish were detected passing the powerhouse in this analysis). The 95-percent confidence intervals of these estimates overlap considerably.

Reach Survival

Survival from the site at the South Fork McKenzie River Bridge to the detection site near Leaburg Hatchery was similar between fish passing via the RO and powerhouse. The estimates were 0.4537 (SE 0.0551) for fish passing through RO and 0.5857 (SE 0.2227) for fish passing through the powerhouse. The standard error is larger for the estimate from the fish passing through the powerhouse due to the low sample size in that category, and the 95-percent confidence intervals of the estimates overlap considerably. These estimates represent a survival per 100 km of 0.1202 for RO fish and 0.2383 for powerhouse fish. The survival estimate over the entire study area from entry into the temperature control tower to the Leaburg Hatchery site 41.2 km downstream was 0.1927 (SE 0.0295) for fish that passed through the RO and 0.2155 (SE 0.1102) for fish that passed through the powerhouse. Once again, the 95-percent confidence intervals overlapped considerably.

Table 4. Estimated passage probabilities and survival probabilities of radio-tagged yearling Chinook salmon passing through the temperature control tower and then the regulating outlet (RO) or powerhouse (PH) at Cougar Dam, Oregon, 2011.

[Fish detected in the Leaburg Dam bypass were omitted from the dataset]

Metric	Period	Route	Estimate	Standard error	95-percent confidence interval	
					lower	upper
Passage probabilities						
	Day	RO	0.8896	0.0617	0.7294	0.9719
		PH	0.1104	0.0617	0.0281	0.2706
	Night	RO	0.9417	0.0175	0.9007	0.9693
		PH	0.0583	0.0175	0.0307	0.0993
	Day	Overall[1]	0.1259	0.0265	0.0802	0.1838
	Night	Overall[1]	0.8741	0.0265	0.8162	0.9198
	Overall[2]	RO	0.9352	0.0172	0.8966	0.9586
		PH	0.0648	0.0172	0.0385	0.1033
Survival probabilities						
Temperature control tower entry to South Fork McKenzie River bridge (3.9 km downstream)						
		RO	0.4247	0.0440	0.3416	0.5138
		PH	0.3680	0.1322	0.1501	0.6371
		Overall[3]	0.4210	0.0420	0.3452	0.5620
South Fork McKenzie River bridge to Leaburg Hatchery (37.3 km)						
		RO	0.4537	0.0551	0.3485	0.5620
		PH	0.5857	0.2227	0.1890	0.9173
Temperature control tower entry to Leaburg Hatchery (41.2 km)						
		RO	0.1927	0.0295	0.1421	0.2550
		PH	0.2155	0.1102	0.0863	0.3885

[1] Pooling data from the RO and PH.

[2] Pooling day and night periods.

[3] Estimated as the joint probability of route-specific passage and survival.

Discussion

The study was conducted during the planned operational conditions of nearly equal discharge through the powerhouse and RO routes. Three fish were omitted from analysis because they passed during operations outside the objective.

The estimate of route-specific passage probability through the RO is higher than previously estimated. Monzyk and others (2011b) estimated route-specific passage probabilities using PIT-tagged fish and detectors in the powerhouse and RO tailraces. They estimated that 51 percent of the tagged fish passed through the RO when 67 percent of a total discharge of 1,590 ft^3/s was passing the RO, and 64.3 percent RO passage when 71.4 percent of a total discharge of 3,780 ft^3/s was passing the RO. We estimated 93.52 percent RO passage when 48.3 percent of a total discharge of 1,106 ft^3/s was passing the RO. Both studies used yearling-sized Chinook salmon, but the fish in this study were of a slightly smaller range (102–166 mm FL) than the 107–208 mm FL range used by Monzyk and others (2011b). Forebay elevations also were similar between studies, being an average of 1,579 ft NGVD29 as fish were first detected in the tailraces in this study, 1,543 ft NGVD29 during one test period of Monzyk and others (2011b), and 1,574 ft NGVD29 in their other test period. Monzyk and others (2011b) discuss several limitations to their study that may have biased their results, including issues with expansion factors and estimation of detection probabilities that may explain the different results from the two studies. In our study, there were tagged fish known to have passed through the dam tailraces without being detected, which required us to use a variation of the RSSM to estimate detection probability through the RO tailrace. The mathematical model we used assigned most of those fish to the RO route, which is consistent with the evidence that tag signal collisions occurred in that route due to the large number of tags there. If that premise was incorrect our estimate of RO passage would be biased upward, but the preponderance of evidence indicates that is unlikely.

Most fish passed the dam during the night. The high passage probability at night was common to fish groups released during the day and those released at night. We estimated that the passage probability at night was 0.8741, which is 6.9 times greater than during the day. The passage timing results from this study, which are based on surface-acclimated fish taken directly from a hatchery and released near the water surface through a hose, are similar to those from fish carrying acoustic tags that had been in the reservoir for weeks and passed volitionally (Beeman and others, 2012b).

Our estimate of the joint probability of entry into the diversion canal and detection by the PIT detector system at Leaburg Dam is theoretically unbiased, but the available evidence indicates that it underrepresents the probability of fish entering the diversion bypass due to reliance on the PIT detection system there as the only detection method. There were 10 study fish captured in the screw trap within the Leaburg bypass downstream of the PIT detector coils that were not detected passing the coils. Our estimate of the joint probability of entering the diversion bypass and detection at the PIT detector therefore underrepresents the probability of fish entry into the diversion bypass because the detection probability of the PIT detector system was less than 1.0. The PIT detection system at the Leaburg diversion was recently upgraded with new detector coils prior to this study, and tests of the system using PIT-tagged fish released within the bypass indicate that the detection probability of the PIT system was approximately 0.5, due partially to ambient noise from a screen cleaner and also periodic power outages (Gordon Axel, National Oceanic and Atmospheric Administration, oral commun., January 13, 2011).

Our estimates of dam-passage survival are lower than might be expected given the results of studies of direct dam-passage survival at Cougar Dam during the winter of 2009–10. The study of survival based on fish carrying balloon tags and radio tags indicated direct RO passage survival 48-h after passage of 88.4 and 88.3 percent during two tests and direct turbine passage survival of 42.4, 36.4, and 37.1 percent during three tests (Monzyk and others, 2011a). Our results reflect estimates of survival over a larger spatial area and include both direct effects (for example, strike, shear, and barotrauma) and indirect effects (for example, predation), as well as mortality that could occur later than 48 h after passage. The spatial area of our estimates is from release directly upstream of the temperature control tower trash rack to the South Fork McKenzie River Bridge 3.9 km downstream of the dam. Our estimate of powerhouse passage survival (0.3680, SE 0.1322) is similar to the balloon tag estimates, but is imprecise due to the small number of fish passing that route.

Our estimate of survival for fish passing the RO route (0.4247, SE 0.0440) is lower than the previous estimates of direct survival. This may be caused by several things, including mortality inside the temperature control tower prior to passage, a true difference in survival during passage through the RO, expression of passage-related mortality downstream of the South Fork McKenzie River bridge, non-passage related factors in that area, and failure of live tagged fish to pass the sites prior to battery expiration (that is, false negatives). High mortality while fish are within the tower seems unlikely, but little is known about that topic. The RO gate opening during this study was smaller than that during the study using balloon tags (1.25 ft versus 1.5 and 3.7 ft), indicating a possible source of lower survival during RO passage. Indirect mortality caused by predation is a plausible source of the low estimates. However, the local sources of predation are not well known. There are few avian predators in the area, but we saw several North American river otters (*Lontra canadensis*) in or near the tailrace. Little is known about the presence and abundance of predaceous fish in the area, but bull trout (*Salvelinus confluentus*) and other salmonids are present in the river system. We have direct evidence that some live fish passed the detection sites with dead radio tags, representing false-negatives that will result in underestimation of survival. Of the three fish detected at PIT sites after the expected life of the radio tags, one was last detected in the RO tailrace and two were last detected at the McKenzie River Bridge. The extent of the bias in our survival estimates from false negatives is likely small, but is unknown.

The reach survival between the South Fork McKenzie River Bridge and the site at Leaburg Hatchery is lower than reach survival in some other river systems. The survival per 100 km between the South Fork McKenzie River Bridge and Leaburg Hatchery was 0.1202 for fish passing through the RO and 0.2383 for those passing through the powerhouse (the estimate from the powerhouse is based on few fish and is the less precise of the two estimates). Estimates of survival per 100 km were 0.790 for yearling coho salmon in the lower Klamath River and 0.639 in the Trinity River in northern California (Beeman and others, 2009, 2012a). Survival of juvenile Chinook salmon per 100 km in the Sacramento River was 0.443 and 0.564 during two periods described by Perry and others (2010). Survival of hatchery juvenile Chinook salmon from hatchery release through the undammed portion of the Snake River to the tailrace of Lower Granite Dam ranged from 0.794 to 0.904 per 100 km (Williams and others, 2005). Thus, reach-survival estimates from this study are lower than in some other river systems. There are two likely factors affecting this result: one is chronic expression of passage-related mortality, and the other is fish living longer than their radio tags. Monzyk and others (2011a) found greater mortality of balloon-tagged fish 48-h after passage than 24-h after passage, indicating that there is a chronic expression of passage-related mortality (at least up to 48 h). In our study, most fish passed the South Fork McKenzie River Bridge site well prior to 48-h, making it likely that passage-related mortality was expressed in reaches downstream of that site. If passage-related mortality was expressed after passage at the South Fork McKenzie River Bridge site, then estimates of in-river survival in reaches downstream would be biased low. There also is evidence that survival was underestimated due to live fish passing sites after the expected battery life of their radio tags. These potential shortcomings could be addressed in future studies by using a paired-release design and using tags with longer life.

The estimates of survival from this study should be evaluated in the context of the model assumptions and limitations of the study. There is a suite of assumptions associated with the mathematical model used to estimate the passage and survival probabilities. One assumption is that the fate of fish is known without error, that is, a live and dead fish can be differentiated from one another. No euthanized fish were detected at downstream sites, indicating that in the data available there was no evidence that dead fish with live tags would be detected after dam passage. It also is possible that live fish with dead tags could pass detection sites undetected, biasing the estimated survival downward. This possibility is often addressed by comparing fish travel times through the study area to tag lives, and in some cases adjusting the estimates of survival using these data (Cowen and Schwarz, 2005). Inasmuch as estimating survival was not the primary purpose of this study, we did not conduct a tag life study, but compared the manufacturer's predicted tag life to fish travel times. The manufacturer's predicted tag life ranged from 13.6 to 16.0 days, depending on the tag repetition rate, which is close to the longest period from tag activation to detection by radio-telemetry equipment at Leaburg Hatchery or McKenzie Hatchery of 12.0 days. However, as discussed previously, three study fish were detected at PIT detectors after the expected radio tag life, providing evidence that this assumption was violated and the estimates of survival contain some amount of downward bias (that is, they are lower than the true value). Radio-telemetry was a useful tool to address the study objectives, but there were limitations. The large number of fish passing through the RO route resulted in collisions of tag signals and a lower detection probability in that area than was expected. This could be alleviated in future studies by allotting tags to a greater number of frequencies, or by using tags with slower repetition rates. If survival were to be estimated in future studies, tags with a longer lives than those used in this study would be an asset.

It has been useful in other areas, such as the Klamath and Sacramento Rivers in California and the lower Columbia River, to partition estimates of in-river survival among several reaches to enable areas with low survival to be identified and the causes evaluated (Beeman, 2007; Perry and others, 2010). This could be done in tributaries of the Willamette River and within the main stem Willamette River using active telemetry techniques.

In summary, radio telemetry was used to estimate several passage and survival probabilities of yearling Chinook salmon that passed through Cougar Dam during November 2011. Dam passage was primarily through the RO and occurred primarily at night. The joint probability of passage into the bypass at the water diversion at Leaburg Dam and detection at the PIT detector there was lower than the probability of fish entering the bypass due to the low detection probability of the PIT detection system there. The single-release dam-passage survival estimate from fish passing through the RO, which represents entry into the temperature control tower to arrival at a site 3.9 km downstream of the dam, was low relative to recent estimates of direct survival and the in-river survival downstream of there was lower than in some other systems. There was evidence that the survival estimates were biased downward from live fish remaining between detection sites longer than the tag life, as indicated by three fish that were detected at the PIT detection sites well after the radio tag batteries were expected to be depleted.

Acknowledgments

Many people assisted with this study. The State of Oregon staff at the McKenzie River Fish Hatchery provided study fish, holding space, and were gracious in allowing us to use their facility. The staff at Cougar Dam assisted us in many aspects of logistics at the site. Ty Hatton, Matt Sholtis, Dana Shurtleff, Jamie Sprando, Nick Swyers, and Ryan Tomka of USGS assisted with field work and data analysis. Scott Fielding of the Portland District U.S. Army Corps of Engineers arranged contracts and provided helpful information and coordination for the study. Funding for this project was provided by the U.S. Army Corps of Engineers, Portland District, Contract W66QKZ11885077.

References Cited

Beeman, J.W., 2007, Summary of survival data from juvenile coho salmon in the Klamath River, northern California, 2006: U.S. Geological Survey Open-File Report 2007-1023, 6 p.

Beeman, J.W., Braatz, A.C., Hansel, H.C., Fielding, S.D., Haner, P.V., Hansen, G.S., Shurtleff, D.J., Sprando, J.M., and Rondorf, D.W., 2010, Approach, passage, and survival of juvenile salmonids at Little Goose Dam, Washington: Post-construction evaluation of a temporary spillway weir, 2009: U.S. Geological Survey Open-File Report 2010-1224, 102 p. .(Also available at http://pubs.usgs.gov/of/2010/1224/.)

Beeman, J.W., Grant, C., and Haner, P.V., 2004, Comparison of three underwater antennas for use in radio telemetry: North American Journal of Fisheries Management, v. 24, p. 275–281.

Beeman, J.W., Hansel, H.C., Hansen, A.C., Haner, P.V., Sprando, J.M., Smith, C.D., and Evans, S.D., 2012b, Interim results from a study of the behavior of juvenile Chinook salmon at Cougar Reservoir and Dam, Oregon: U.S. Geological Survey Open-File Report 2012-1106, 30 p. (Also available at http://pubs.usgs.gov/of/2012/1106/.)

Beeman, J.W., Hansel, H., Juhnke, S., and Stutzer, G., 2009, Summary of migration and survival data from radio-tagged juvenile coho salmon in the Trinity River, northern California, 2008: U.S. Geological Survey Open-File Report 2009-1092, 26 p. (Also available at *http://pubs.usgs.gov/of/2009/1092/.*)

Beeman, J., Juhnke, S., Stutzer, G., and Wright, K., 2012a, Effects of Iron Gate Dam discharge and other factors on the survival and migration of juvenile coho salmon in the Klamath River, Northern California: U.S. Geological Survey Open-File Report 2012-1067, 96 p. (Also available at *http://pubs.usgs.gov/of/2012/1067/.*)

Beeman, J.W., and Perry, R.W., 2012, Bias from false-positive detections and strategies for their removal in studies using telemetry, *in* N.S. Adams, J.W. Beeman, and Eiler, J.H., eds., Telemetry techniques: A user guide for fisheries research: Bethesda, Maryland, American Fisheries Society, p. 505–518.

Burnham, K.P., Anderson, D.R., White, G.C., Brownie, C., and Pollock, K.H., 1987, Design and analysis methods for fish survival experiments based on release-recapture: Bethesda, Maryland, American Fisheries Society, America Fisheries Society Monograph 5, 737 p.

Cowen, L., and Schwarz, C.J., 2005, Capture-recapture studies using radio telemetry with premature radio-tag failure: Biometrics, v. 61, p. 657–664.

Duncan, J.P, 2011, Characterization of fish passage conditions through a Francis turbine and regulating outlet at Cougar Dam, Oregon, using sensor fish, 2009–2010: Pacific Northwest Laboratory report PNNL-20408, 172 p.

Hosmer, D.W., Jr., and Lemeshow, S., 1999, Applied survival analysis: regression modeling of time to event data: New York, John Wiley and Sons, 386 p.

Jolly, G.M., 1965, Explicit estimates from capture-recapture data with both death and immigration-stochastic model: Biometrika, v. 52, no. 1/2, p. 225–247.

Lady, J.M., and Skalski, J.R., 2009, USER 4: User-specified estimation routine: Prepared for U.S. Department of Energy, Bonneville Power Administration, Portland, Oregon, Project No. 198910700, Portland, Oregon, 45 p., accessed October 25, 2012, at *http://www.cbr.washington.edu/paramest/user/*.

Monzyk, F., Heisey, P., Duncan, J., and Griffith, D., 2011a, Draft executive summary to Willamette Action Team for Restoration, preliminary results for 2009–2010 downstream passage studies at Cougar Dam: Report to U.S. Army Corps of Engineers, Portland, Oregon, 22 p.

Monzyk, F.R., Hogansen, M., Romer, J.D. , and Friesen, T.S., 2011b, Cougar Dam route selection study, evaluating fish passage using spill: Report to U.S. Army Corps of Engineers, Contract W9127N-10-2-0008, Portland, Oregon, 15 p.

National Oceanic and Atmospheric Administration, 2008, Endangered Species Act section 7(a)(2) consultation biological opinion & Magnuson-Stevens Fishery Conservation & Management Act essential fish habitat consultation: Consultation on the "Willamette River Basin Flood Control Project", NOAA Fisheries Log Number: FINWRl2000/02117, June 11, 2008, accessed October 25, 2012, at *http://www.nwr.noaa.gov/Salmon-Hydropower/Willamette-Basin/Willamette-BO.cfm*.

Perry, R.W., Skalski, J.R., Brandes, P.L., Sandstrom, P.T., Klimley, A.P., Ammann, A., and MacFarlane, B., 2010, Estimating survival and migration route probabilities of juvenile Chinook salmon in the Sacramento-San Joaquin river delta: North American Journal of Fisheries Management, v. 30, p. 142-156.

Seber, G.A.F., 1965, A note on the multiple recapture census: Biometrika, v. 52, no. 1/2. p. 249–259.

Skalski, J.R., Townsend, R., Lady, J., Giorgi, A.E., Stevenson, J.R., and McDonald, R.S., 2002, Estimating route-specific passage and survival probabilities at a hydroelectric project from smolt radiotelemetry studies: Canadian Journal of Fisheries and Aquatic Sciences, v. 59, p. 1385–1393.

Surgical Protocol Steering Committee, 2011, Surgical protocols for implanting JSATS transmitters into juvenile salmonids for studies conducted for the U.S. Army Corps of Engineers: Report prepared by Surgical Protocols Steering Committee for U.S. Army Corps of Engineers, Portland, Oregon, 18 p.

Williams, J.G., Smith, S.G., Zabel, R.W., Muir, W.D., Scheuerell, M.D., Sandford, B.P., Marsh, D.M., McNatt, R.A., and Achord, S., 2005, Effects of the federal Columbia River power system on salmonid populations: U.S. Department of Commerce, NOAA Technical Memorandum NMFS-NWFSC-63, 150 p.

Appendix A. Schematic of the mathematical model used to estimate route-specific passage and survival probabilities

Detection arrays (P), Turbine (Tur), and regulating outlet (Ro) are shown. P_{tur} = probability of detecting a fish passing the turbines; P_{ro} = probability of detecting a fish passing the regulating outlet; TurSr1 = probability of survival from turbine passage to the first downstream detection gate; RoSr1 = probability of survival from regulating outlet passage to the first downstream detection gate; TurSr2 = probability of survival of fish passing the turbines from the McKenzie Bridge to Leaburg Hatchery; RoSr2 = probability of survival of fish passing the RO from the McKenzie Bridge to Leaburg Hatchery, λ = lambda.

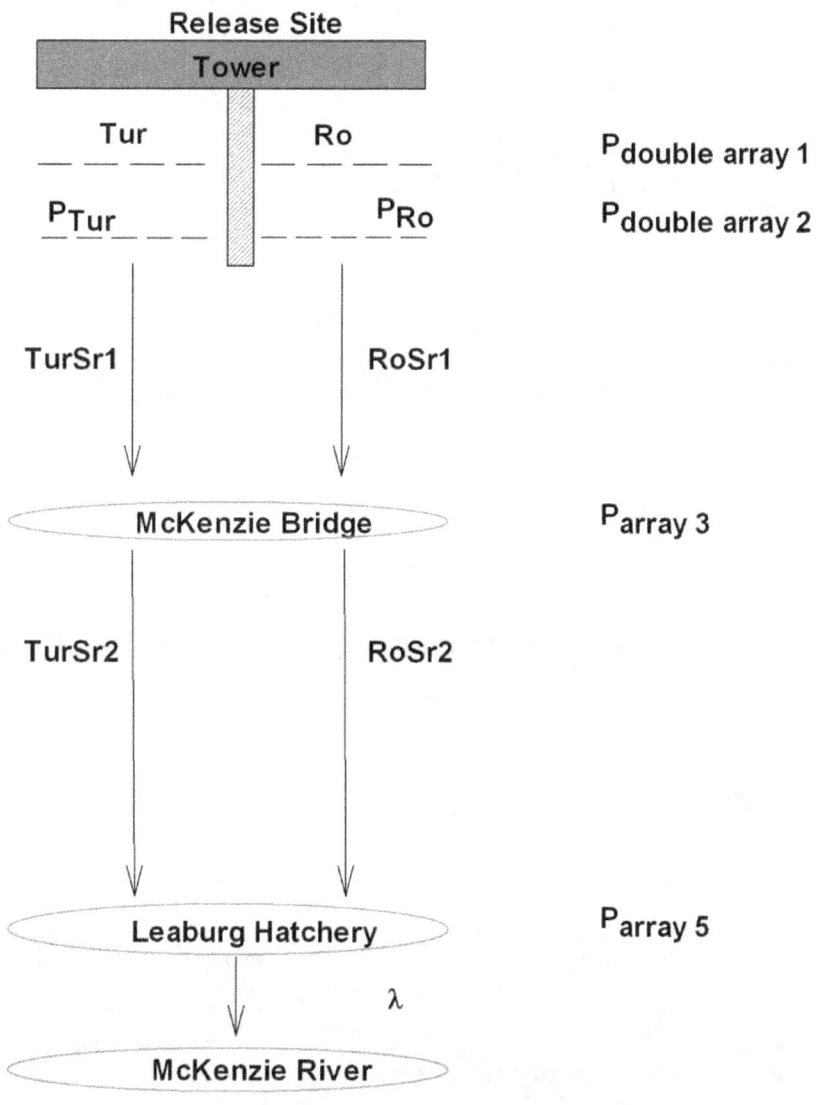

Appendix B. Schematic of the mathematical model used to estimate the joint probability of entering the Leaburg Dam bypass and being detected by the PIT detector within it

      Detection arrays (P) and survival reaches used to estimate the probability of entering the PIT-tag detector (P $_{pit\ tag\ array\ 4}$) at Leaburg Dam are shown. Tur = turbines; Ro = regulating outlet; P$_{tur}$ = probability of detecting a fish passing the turbines; P$_{ro}$ = probability of detecting a fish passing the regulating outlet; TurSr1 = probability of survival from turbine passage to the first downstream detection gate; RoSr1 = probability of survival from regulating outlet passage to the first downstream detection gate; Sr2 = probability of survival from the first survival gate to Leaburg Dam; Sr3 = probability of survival from Leaburg PIT detector to Leaburg Hatchery, λ = lambda.

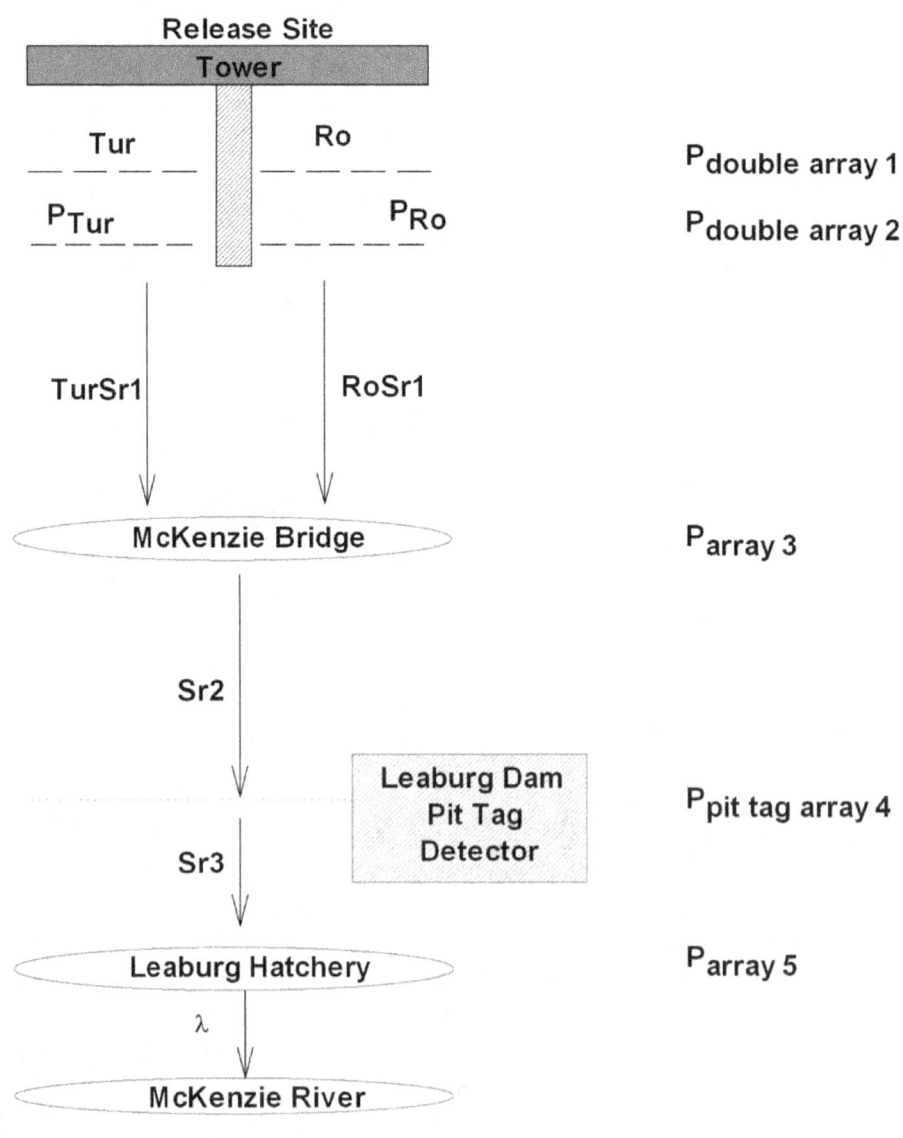

Appendix C. Detection history counts for radio-tagged yearling Chinook salmon used to estimate passage and survival probabilities at Cougar Dam, Oregon, November 2011

[See table 1 for detection history definition]

Passage Route	Detection History	Photoperiod			Double Arrays		
		Light	Dark	Total	Array 1	Array 2	Array 1 & 2
Turbines	1PH111	0	2	2	2	2	10
	1PH100	0	2	2			
	1PH001	0	0	0			
	1PH110	0	0	0			
	1PH011	0	0	0			
	1PH000	3	6	9			
	1PH101	0	1	1			
	1PH010	0	0	0			
Regulating Outlet	1RO111	2	21	23			
	1RO100	6	26	32			
	1RO001	0	0	0			
	1RO110	0	0	0			
	1RO011	1	0	1			
	1RO000	8	76	84			
	1RO101	0	2	2			
	1RO010	0	0	0			
Unknown	1UN111	na	na	9			
	1UN100	na	na	13			
	1UN001	na	na	0			
	1UN110	na	na	1			
	1UN011	na	na	2			
	1UN000	na	na	60			
	1UN101	na	na	2			
	1UN010	na	na	0			

Appendix D. Detection history counts for radio-tagged fish passing through the turbines, regulating outlet, or with an unknown route of passage used to estimate the probability of entrance and detection at the PIT-tag collector at Leaburg Dam, Oregon, November 2011.

[See table 1 for detection history definition]

Passage Route	Detection History	Photoperiod			Double Arrays		
		Light	Dark	Total	Array 1	Array 2	Array 1 & 2
Turbines	1PH1111	0	1	1	2	2	12
	1PH1110	0	0	0			
	1PH1101	0	0	0			
	1PH1100	0	0	0			
	1PH1011	0	3	3			
	1PH1010	0	0	0			
	1PH1001	0	1	1			
	1PH1000	0	2	2			
	1PH0111	0	0	0			
	1PH0110	0	0	0			
	1PH0101	0	0	0			
	1PH0100	0	0	0			
	1PH0011	0	0	0			
	1PH0010	0	0	0			
	1PH0001	0	0	0			
	1PH0000	3	6	9			
Regulating Outlet	1RO1111	0	1	1			
	1RO1110	1	0	1			
	1RO1101	0	0	0			
	1RO1100	0	2	2			
	1RO1011	3	22	25			
	1RO1010	0	0	0			
	1RO1001	0	4	4			
	1RO1000	7	28	35			
	1RO0111	0	0	0			
	1RO0110	0	0	0			
	1RO0101	0	0	0			
	1RO0100	0	1	1			
	1RO0011	1	0	1			
	1RO0010	0	0	0			
	1RO0001	0	0	0			
	1RO0000	8	76	84			
Unknown	1UN1111	na	na	1			
	1UN1110	na	na	0			
	1UN1101	na	na	0			
	1UN1100	na	na	0			
	1UN1011	na	na	10			
	1UN1010	na	na	1			
	1UN1001	na	na	2			
	1UN1000	na	na	13			
	1UN0111	na	na	0			
	1UN0110	na	na	0			
	1UN0101	na	na	0			
	1UN0100	na	na	1			
	1UN0011	na	na	2			
	1UN0010	na	na	0			
	1UN0001	na	na	0			
	1UN0000	na	na	61			

www.ingramcontent.com/pod-product-compliance
Lightning Source LLC
Chambersburg PA
CBHW080355290526
45791CB00009BA/2884